# Introducing
# Teddy Spaghetti

## BY DIANE ZIZZO

### ILLUSTRATIONS BY EARLENE GAYLE ESCALONA

I want to thank my wonderful husband, Phil
& my two great sons, Joe & Mike for
their encouragement & love.

Hi there, My name is Teddy
And I reeaally love spaghetti.
That's why everyone calls me
"Teddy Spaghetti"!

I really like my morning walks
To listen to the birds
They sing so many different songs
But not one I've ever heard

Today I saw a butterfly
And while watching where it goes
It flew around, then flew by me
And landed on my nose!

Here's Grandma with a treat
She says "O.K. get ready!!!"
I hope it's what I think it is
IT IS!...she brought spaghetti

So I guess now its time for my haircut
Because I can hardly see
The groomer cut my fluffy hair
Ruff! This is a cute looking me!

I love to take car rides with daddy
I stick out my head in the breeze
When the car ride is over, I keep asking
"Can we do that again daddy please?"

Finally at the dog park to meet all my friends
Where we really like to dig.
One day a new friend came walking in.
He wasn't a dog but a pig!!

I said "Hi, my name is Teddy,
Do you like spaghetti?
He said "Yes" so we all got ready
To share a big bowl of spaghetti.

I had such fun with all my friends,
"Penny", "Miller", and "Clive",
"Madison", "Duke" & Honey too
We said good-bye & slapped high five!

I'm a good boy when it nap time
My Mommy tells me this.
I go to bed and lay right down
And she gives me a great BIG kiss

I love my two big brothers,
And I know that they love me
We play and wrestle all the time.
They are fun as fun can be!

I have a real nice Uncle.
He's lots and lots of fun
Whenever he takes me for a walk
All we really do is run

I watch my daddy mow the lawn
He makes it neat and clean
Then I go and roll on it,
And my nice white fur turns GREEN!!

Then I hear my Mommy say..
"Teddy, supper is ready.
Can you guess what we'll be eating?
YOU'RE RIGHT!! I made spaghetti!!

I love to hear "It's bathtime".
I run right to the tub
It's all filled up with bubbles
Then I get a bubbly scrub!

Daddy says "It's time for bed"
Then hugs me very tight
Mommy gives me kisses
And then they say "Good-Night"

Our Little "Teddy Spaghetti"

"Night Night"

Draw Teddy a friend here.

Draw your pet here.